I0011574

Book 1
C++ Programming Professional Made Easy

BY SAM KEY

&

Book 2
Excel Shortcuts

BY SAM KEY

Book 1
C++ Programming Professional Made Easy

BY SAM KEY

Expert C++ Programming Language Success in a Day for Any Computer User!

Programming Box Set #55: C++ Programming Professional Made Easy & Excel Shortcuts

Table Of Contents

Introduction

I want to thank you and congratulate you for purchasing the book, "Professional C++ Programming Made Easy".

This book contains proven steps and strategies on how to learn the C++ programming language as well as its applications.

There's no need to be a professional developer to code quick and simple C++ programs. With this book, anyone with basic computer knowledge can explore and enjoy the power of the *C++ Programming Language*. Included are the following fundamental topics for any beginner to start coding *today:*

- The basic C++ terms
- Understanding the C++ Program Structure
- Working with Variables, Expressions, and Operators
- Using the Input and Output Stream for User Interaction
- Creating Logical Comparisons
- Creating Loops and Using Condition Statements
- And Many More!

Thanks again for purchasing this book, I hope you enjoy it!

Chapter 1 – Introduction to C++

What You Will Learn:

***A Brief History of the C++ Language*

***C++ Basic Terminology*

***C++ Program Structure*

C++ is one of the most popular programming languages that people are using today. More specifically, C++ is a library of "commands" that tell your computer what to do and how to do it. These commands make up the *C++ source code.*

Take note that C++ is different from the *C* programming language that came before it. In fact, it is supposedly better version of the C language when *Bjarne Stroustrup* created it back in 1983.

Even today, the C++ language serves as the "starting point" for many experts in the world of programming. Although it is particularly easy to learn and apply, the ceiling for C++ mastery is incredibly high.

C++ Basic Terminology

Of course, the first step in learning the C++ programming language is to understand the basic terms. To prevent any unnecessary confusion at any point as you read this book, this section explains the most commonly used terms in the C++ program syntax. Just like the entire programming language itself, most terms in C++ are easy to remember and understand.

Compiler

Before anything else, take note that a compiler is needed to run the codes you've written with C++. Think of compilers as "translators" that convert programming language into *machine language* – the language that a computer understands. The machine language consists of only two characters (1s and 0s), which is why it is also called as *binary language.* If you're learning C++ at school, then you shouldn't worry about getting a compiler for C++ *or* an *Integrated Development Environment* for that matter.

Integrated Development Environment

An Integrated Development Environment (IDE) is essentially the software you're using to write C++ programs. It only makes sense for IDEs to come with compilers needed to run your codes. If you have no experience with C++ programming and attempting to learn it on your own, you can opt for a free C++ IDE such as *Code::Blocks.* A good choice for complete beginners is to opt for a simple C++ IDE such as *Quincy 2005* since there is very little setup required.

Variables and Parameters

Variables are individual blocks in the program's memory that contains a given value. A value may be set as a constant, determined by the value of other variables using operators, or set/changed through user input. Variables are denoted by variable names or *identifiers.* In programming with C++, you can use any variable name you desire as long as all characters are valid. Remember that only alphanumeric characters and "underscores" (_) can be used in identifiers. Punctuation marks and other symbols are not allowed.

Keep in mind that variables always need to be *declared* first before they can be used. Declaring variables are different from deciding their actual values; meaning both processes are done in two different codes. These processes will be explained in the next chapter.

"Parameters" work the same way as regular variables. In fact, they are even written in the same syntax. However, parameters and variables are initialized in different ways. Parameters are specifically included in *functions* to allow arguments to be passed to a separate location from which the functions are called.

Statements

Every program written with C++ consists of different lines of code that performs tasks such as setting variables, calling functions, and other expressions. These lines are *statements.* Each individual statement always ends with a semicolon (;). More importantly, statements in a function are executed chronologically based on which comes first. Of course, this order can be altered using *flow control statements* such as “if statements” and “loops”.

Functions

Functions are blocks in a C++ program structured to complete a single task. You can call upon functions at any point whilst the program is running. Curly brackets or braces ({}) enclose the statements or “body” in each function. Aside from a function name, functions are also set with corresponding “types” which refer to the requested form of *returned value.* You can also use and set parameters at the beginning of each function. They are enclosed in parentheses “()” and separated using commas (,).

In C++, the following is the most used syntax when creating functions:

```
“type” “name” ( parameter 1, parameter 2, parameter 3, ...)
{
        “statements”;
}
```

Comments

When working on particularly bigger projects, most experienced programmers use “comments” that can be used as descriptions for specific sections in a C++ program. Comments are completely ignored by a compiler and can therefore ignore proper coding syntax. Comments are preceded either by a *two slashes* (//) or a *slash-asterisk* (/*). You will find comments in the examples throughout this book to help you understand them. A quick example would be the “*Hello World!*” program below. Of course, you can also use comments in your future projects for reference and debugging purposes.

The C++ Program Structure

The program structure of C++ is very easy to understand. The compiler reads every line of code from top to bottom. This is why the first part of a C++ program usually starts with *preprocessor directives* and the declaration of variables and their values. The best way to illustrate this structure is to use the most popular example in the world of C++ -- the "Hello World!" program. Take note of the lines of code as well as the comments below:

#include <iostream> // this is a preprocessor directive

int main() // this line initiates the function named main, which should be found in every C++ program

{

> **std::cout << "Hello World!";** // the statements found between the curly braces make up the main function's body
>
> **return 0;** // the return 0; statement is required to tell the program that the function ran correctly. However, some compilers do not require this line in the main function

}

The topmost line ("#include <iostream>") is a preprocessor directive that defines a section of the standard C++ programming library known as the Input/Output Stream or simply *iostream*. This section handles the input and output operations in C++ programs. Remember that this is important if you wish to use "std::cout" in the main function's body.

The first line "int main ()" initializes the main function. Remember that the "int" refers to the *integer* data type and he "main" refers to the function's name. There are other data types aside from int. But you should focus on the integer data type for now. Since the "Hello World!" program does not need a parameter, it leaves the space between the parentheses succeeding the function name blank. Also, bear in mind that you should NOT place a semicolon (;) after initializing functions.

Next is the function's body, denoted by the open curly brace. This particular part ("std::cout") of the program refers to the **st**andar**d** **c**haracter **out**put device, which is the computer's display device. Next comes the *insertion operator* (<<) from the input/output stream which means the rest of the line is to be outputted (excluding quotations). Lastly, the statement is closed with a semicolon (;).

The last line in the function's body is the *return statement* ("return = 0;"). Remember that the return expression (in this example, "0") depends on the data type specified upon initialization of the function. However, it is possible to create functions without the need for return statements using the "void" function type. For example; *void main ().*

An alternate way to do this is to include the line "using namespace std;" under the preprocessor line so you no longer need to write "std::" each time you use it. If you opt for this method, the code would look like:

```
#include <iostream>

using namespace std;

int main()

{

        cout << "Hello World!";

        return 0;

}
```

Chapter 2 – C++ Variables and Operators

What You Will Learn:

***Introduction to C++ Operators and How to Use Them*

***Declaring and Determining the Value of Variables*

***Creating New Lines in the Program Output*

In a C++ program, variables and constants are controlled or "operated" using *Operators*. Take note that the basic operators in the C++ programming language are essentially the same as arithmetic operator. This includes the equal sign (=) for assigning expressions, the plus sign (+) for addition, the minus sign (-) for subtraction, the asterisk (*) for multiplication, the forward slash (/) for division, and the percentage sign (%) for obtaining the remainder from any expression.

C++ also uses other operators to fulfill additional tasks other than basic arithmetic operations. As mentioned in the previous chapter, the iostream header allowed you to use the insertion operator (<<) for processing output. There are also different operators accessible even without the #include directive. These "basic" operators can be categorized under *increment/decrement operators, comparison operators, compound assignment operators,* and *logical operators.*

Declaring Variables

Before using variables in C++ operations, you must first declare them and determine their values. Again, declaring variables and giving their values are two separate processes. The syntax for declaring variables are as follows:

"type" "variable";

Just like when initializing functions, you need to specify the data type to be used for a given variable. For example; say you want to declare "x" as an integer variable. The initialization should look like this:

```
int x;
```

After the declaration of x, you can give it a value using the assign operator (=). For example; to assign the value "99" to variable x, use the following line:

```
x = 99;
```

Make sure to declare a variable first before you assign a value to it. Alternatively, you can declare a variable and assign a value to it using a single line. This can be done using:

```
int x = 99;
```

Aside from setting these expressions as you write the program, you can also use operations and user input to determine their values as the program runs. But first, you need to learn about the other operators in C++.

Increment and Decrement Operators

The increment operator consists of two plus signs (++) while the decrement operator consists of two minus signs (--). The main purpose of increment and decrement operators is to shorten the expression of adding and subtracting 1 from any given variable. For example; if x = 2, then ++x should equal 3 while –x should equal 1.

If being used to determine the values of two or more variables, increment and decrement operators can be included as either a prefix or suffix. When used as a suffix (x++ or x--), it denotes the original value of x *before* adding or subtracting 1. When run on their own, both ++x and x++ have the same meaning. But when used in setting other variables, the difference is made obvious. Here is a simple example to illustrate the difference:

```
X = 5;
```

Y = ++x;

In this example, the value of y is determined *after* increasing the value of x. In other words, the value of y in this example is equal to 6.

X = 5;

Y = x++;

In this example, the value of y is determined *before* increasing the value of x. In other words, the value of y in this example is equal to 6.

Compound Assignment Operators

Aside from basic arithmetic operators and the standard assignment operator (=), compound assignment operators can also be used to perform an operation before a value is assigned. Compound assignment operators are basically shortened versions of normal expressions that use basic arithmetic operators.

Here are some examples of compound assignment operators:

x -= 1; // this is the same as the expression x = x – 1;

x *= y; // this is the same as the expression x = x * y;

x += 1;   // this is the same as the expression x = x + 1;

x /= y;   // this is the same as the expression x = x / y;

Comparison Operators

Variables and other expressions can be compared using relational or comparison operators. These operators are used to check whether a value is greater than, less than, or equal to another. Here are the comparison operators used in C++ and their description:

== - checks if the values are equal

< - checks if the first value is less than the second

> - checks if the first value is greater than the second

<= - checks if the first value is less than *or* equal to the second

>= - checks if the first value is greater than *or* equal to the second

!= - checks if the values are NOT equal

Comparison operators are commonly used in creating condition statements. They can also be used to evaluate an expression and return a *Boolean value* ("true" or "false"). Using the comparison operators listed above; here are some example expressions and their corresponding Boolean value:

```
(8 == 1) // this line evaluates to "false"
(8 > 1)  // this line evaluates to "true"
(8 != 1) // this line evaluates to "true"
(8 <= 1) // this line evaluates to "false"
```

Also take note that the Boolean value "false" is equivalent to "0" while "true" is equivalent to other non-zero integers.

Aside from numerical values, the value of variables can also be checked when using comparison operators. Simply use a variable's identifier when creating the expression. Of course, the variable must be declared and given an identified value first before a valid comparison can be made. Here is an example scenario

```
#include <iostream>
using namespace std;

int main ()

{
        int a = 3;      // the values of a and b are set first
        int b = 4;
        cout << "Comparison a < b = " << (a < b);
        return 0;
}
```

The output for this code is as follows:

Comparison a < b = true

Take note that the insertion operator (<<) is used to insert the value of the expression “a < b” in the output statement, which is denoted in the 7th line (“cout << “Comparison a < b = “…). Don’t forget that you *need an output statement* in order to see if your code works. The following code will produce no errors, but it won’t produce an output either:

```
#include <iostream>

int main (

{
        int a = 3;
        int b = 4;
        (a < b);
        return 0;
}
```

In this code, it is also true that a < b. However, no output will be produced since the lines necessary for the program output are omitted.

Logical Operators

There are also other logical operators in C++ that can determine the values of Boolean data. They are the NOT (!), AND (&&), and OR (||) operators. Here are specific examples on how they are used:

!(6 > 2) // the **NOT** operator (!) completely reverses any relational expressions and produces the opposite result. This expression is false because 6 > 2 is correct

(6 > 2 && 5 < 10) // the **AND** (&&) operator only produces true if both expressions correct. This expression is true because both 6 > 2 && 5 < 10 are correct

(6 = 2 || 5 < 10) // the **OR** (||) operator produces true if one of the expressions are correct. This expression is true because the 5 < 10 is correct although 6 = 2 is false.

You can also use the NOT operator in addition to the other two logical operators. For example:

!(6 = 2 || 5 < 10) // this expression is false

!(6 > 2 && 5 < 10) // this expression is also false

!(6 < 2 && 5 < 10) // this expression is true

Creating New Lines

From this point on in this book, you will be introduced to simple C++ programs that produce output with multiple lines. To create new lines when producing output, all you need to do is to use the *new line character* (\n). Alternatively, you can use the "endl;" manipulator to create new lines when using the "cout" code. The main difference is that the *internal buffer* for the output stream is "flushed" whenever you use the "endl;" manipulator with "cout". Here are examples on how to use both:

cout << "Sentence number one \nSentence number two";

The example above uses the new line character.

cout << "Sentence number one" << endl;
cout << "Sentence number two";

The example above uses "endl;".

Of course, the first code (using \n) is relatively simpler and easier for general output purposes. Both will produce the following output:

Sentence number one

Sentence number two

Chapter 3 – All About User Input

What You Will Learn:

***Utilizing the Input Stream*

***Using Input to Determine or Modify Values*

***How to Input and Output Strings*

Up to this point, you've learned how to make a C++ program that can perform arithmetic operations, comparisons, and can produce output as well. This time, you will learn how to code one of the most important aspects of computer programs – *user input.*

As stated earlier, user input can be utilized to determine or modify the values of certain variables. C++ programs use abstractions known as *streams* to handle input and output. Since you already know about the syntax for output ("cout"), it's time to learn about the syntax for input ("cin").

The Extraction Operator

The input syntax "cin" is used with the *extraction operator* (>>) for formatted input. This combination along with the *keyboard* is the standard input for most program environments. Remember that you still need to declare a variable first before input can be made. Here is a simple example:

int x; // this line declares the variable identifier x. Take note of the data type "int" which means that only an integer value is accepted

cin >> x; // this line extracts input from the cin syntax and stores it to x

User input can also be requested for multiple variables in a single line. For example; say you want to store integer values for variables x and y. This should look like:

```
int x, y;      // this line declares the two variables

cin >> x >> y;      // this line extracts user input for variables x and y
```

Take note that the program will automatically require the user to input *two* values for the two variables. Which comes first depends on the order of the variables in the line (in this case, input for variable “x” is requested first).

Here is an example of a program that extracts user input and produces an output:

```
#include <iostream>    // again, this is essential for input and output
using namespace std;

int main ()

{
        int x;
        cout << “Insert a random number \n”;
        cin >> x;    // this is where user input is extracted
        cout << “You inserted: “ << x;
        return 0;

}
```

Bear in mind that the value extracted from the input stream overwrites any initial value of a variable. For example, if the variable was declared as “int x = 2;” but was later followed by the statement “cin >> x;”, the new value will then replace the original value until the program/function restarts or if an assignment statement is introduced.

Strings

Keep in mind that there are other types you can assign to variables in C++. Aside from integers, another fundamental type is the *string*. A string is basically a variable type that can store sets of characters in a specific sequence. In other words, this is how you can assign words or sentences as values for certain variables.

First of all, you need to add the preprocessor directive "#include <string>" before you can use strings in your program. Next, you need to declare a string before it can receive assignments. For example; if you want to declare a string for "Name" and assign a value for it, you can use the code:

```
#include <string>
using namespace std;

int main ()

{
  string name;
  name = "Insert your name here"; // including quotations

}
```

Creating output using strings is basically the same as with integers. You only need to use "cout" and insert the string to the line. The correct syntax is as follows:

```
string name;

Name = "Your Name Here";

cout << "My name is: " << name;
```

Without any changes, the output for the above code is:

Your Name Here

Inputting Strings

To allow user input values for strings, you need to use the function “getline” in addition to the standard input stream “cin”. The syntax for this is “getline (cin, [string]);”. Below is an example program that puts string input into application.

```
#include <iostream>
#include <string>
using namespace std;

int main ()

{
        string name;
        cout << “Greetings! What is your name?\n”;
        getline (cin, name); // this is the extraction syntax
        cout << “Welcome “ << name;
        return 0;

}
```

Take note that strings have “blank” values by default. This means nothing will be printed if no value is assigned or if there is no user input.

Chapter 4 – Using Flow Control Statements

What You Will Learn:

***If and Else Selection Statements*

***Creating Choices*

***Creating Iterating/Looping Statements*

Remember that statements are the basic building blocks of a program written using C++. Each and every line that contains expressions such as a variable declaration, an operation, or an input extraction is a statement.

However, these statements are *linear* without some form of flow control that can establish the "sense" or "logic" behind a C++ program. This is why you should learn how to utilize flow control statements such as *selection statements* and *looping statements.*

If and Else Statements

If and else statements are the most basic form of logic in a C++ program. Basically, the main purpose of an "if" statement is to allow the execution of a specific line or "block" of multiple statements only *if* a specified condition is fulfilled.

Next is the "else" statement which allows you to specify what would occur in case the conditions aren't met. Without an "else" statement, everything inside the "if" statement will be completely ignored. Here the syntax for an "if" and "else" statement:

```
if (age >= 18)
        cout << "You are allowed to drink.";
```

```
else
        cout << "You are not yet allowed to drink.";
```

Remember that conditions can only be set using comparison operators and logical operators (refer to Chapter 2). Take note that you can also execute multiple statements using if/else conditions by enclosing the lines in curly braces. It is also possible to use composite conditions using logical operators such as AND (&&) and OR (||).

Finally, you can use another "if" statement after an "else" statement for even more possibilities. Of course, you also need to specify conditions for every "if" statement you use. Here is a good example that demonstrates what you can do using "if" and "else" statements in addition to user input:

```
#include <iostream>
using namespace std;

int main()

{
        int number;
        cout << "Enter a number from 1-3\n";
        cin >> number;
        if (number == 1 || number == 2)
                cout << "You have entered either 1 or 2.";
        else if (number == 3)
                cout << "You have entered 3.";
        else
        {
                cout << "Please follow the instructions\n";
                cout << "Please Try Again.";
        }
        return 0;
}
```

There are 3 possible outcomes in the program above. The first outcome is achieved if the user entered any of the numbers 1 or 2. The second outcome is achieved if the user entered the number 3. Lastly, the third outcome is achieved if the user entered a different number other the ones specified.

Creating Choices (Yes or No)

Another way to utilize if/else statements is to create “Yes or No” choices. For this, you need to make use of the variable type “char” which can hold a character from the *8-bit character set* (you can use char16_t, char32_t, or wchar_t for larger character sets; but this is not usually necessary). Just like all other variables, a “char” variable needs to be declared before it can be used.

Of course, you want the user to make the choice, which is why you need to use the “cin” function to extract user input. Here is a simple program that asks for the user’s gender:

```
#include <iostream>
using namespace std;

int main()

{
        char gender; // this is the char variable declaration
        cout << “Male or Female? (M/F)”;
        cin >> gender; // user input is stored to gender
        if (gender == ‘m’ || gender == ‘M’)
                cout << “You have selected Male.”;
        else if (gender == ‘f’ || gender == ‘F’)
                cout << “You have selected Female.”;
        else
                cout << “Please follow the instructions.”;
        return 0;

}
```

Take note that you should use *single quotation marks* (‘) when pinpointing “char” values. In C++, “char” values are always called inside single quotation marks. Additionally, remember that “char” values are case-sensitive, which is why the example above used the OR (||) operator in the conditions to accept both lowercase and uppercase answers. You can see that the program above checked if the user entered ‘m’, ‘M’, ‘f’, or ‘F’.

Looping Statements

Lastly, using “loops” allow statements to be executed for a set number of times or until a condition is met. By incorporating other statements in loops, you can do far more than just create pointless repetitions. But first, you need to be familiar with the different types of loops.

There are 3 types of loops in C++ -- *while, do,* and *for.*

While Loop

The *“while loop”* is regarded as the simplest form of loop in the C++. Basically, it repeats the statement(s) as long as the given condition is true. Keep in mind that your code should be structured to eventually fulfill the condition; otherwise you might create an “infinite loop”.

Here is an example of a while loop:

```
int x = 100;

while (x >= 0)      // the condition for the loop is set
      {
      cout << x;
      --x;    // the value of x is decreased
      }
```

In this example, the loop executes as long as the value of x is greater than or equal to 0. Take note of the decrement operator (--) in the statement “--x;”. This makes sure that the value of x is continually decreased until the condition is met and the loop ends.

Do-While Loop

The next type of loop is the "*do-while loop*". The do-while loop is essentially the same as the while loop. The main difference is that the do-while loop allows the execution of the statement(s) at least *once* before the condition is checked. Whereas in the while loop, the condition is checked *first.*

Here is an example of a do-while loop:

```
int x = 100;
int y;

do
        {
        cout << "The value is " << x << "\n";
        cout << "Enter a value to subtract.";
        cin >> y;
        x -= y;
        }
while (x > 0);        // in the do-while loop, the condition is checked last
```

In the example above, the statements are executed at least once before the value of x is checked. Whereas in a while loop, there is a possibility that the statement(s) will not be executed at all.

For Loop

The third type of loop is the *"for loop"* which has specific areas for the *initialization, condition,* and *increase.* These three sections are sequentially executed throughout the life cycle of the loop. By structure, for loops are created to run a certain number of times because increment or decrement operators are usually used in the "increase" section.

Here is the syntax for this loop to help you understand it better:

```
for (int x = 10; x > 0; x--)
```

Notice the three expressions inside the parentheses (int x = 10; x > 0; x--) are separated in semicolons. These parameters denote the three sections of the loop. You may also use multiple expressions for each section using a comma (,). Here is the syntax for this:

```
for ( int x = 10, y = 0; x != y; --x, ++y )
        {
        cout << "X and Y is different\n";
        }
```

In this example, the loop is executed as long as x is not equal to y. And in order for the loop to end, the values of x and y are adjusted until the value of x equals the value of y. Based on the parameters above, the statement "X and Y is different" will run a total of 5 times before the loop is ended.

Conclusion

Thank you again for purchasing this book!

I hope this book was able to help you to learn and understand the C++ programming language!

The next step is to start from where you are now and try to learn something new. Keep in mind that you've only scratched the surface of all the things you can do in the world of C++!

Finally, if you enjoyed this book, please take the time to share your thoughts and post a review on Amazon. We do our best to reach out to readers and provide the best value we can. Your positive review will help us achieve that. It'd be greatly appreciated!

Thank you and good luck!

Book 2

Excel Shortcuts

BY SAM KEY

The 100 Top Best Powerful Excel Keyboard Shortcuts in 1 Day!

Table Of Contents

Introduction

I want to thank you and congratulate you for purchasing the book, "The Power of Excel Shortcuts: The 100 Top Best Powerful Excel Keyboard Shortcuts in 1 Day!".

This book contains proven steps and strategies on how to master the Microsoft Excel through just 100 keyboard shortcuts! However, most people will ask, "Why do you need to learn these shortcuts anyway?"

Advantages of Using Microsoft Excel

Microsoft Excel has become one of the most commonly used enterprise software in schools and offices. Its way of presenting data, which is through a spreadsheet, has helped a lot of people especially in the field of data mining. If you were going to put numerous rows of data, in let's say, a word processing program, it might take a lot of time creating tables and formatting each of them to fit in the pages. With the Microsoft Excel, these manual tasks are now much easier.

What does the Microsoft Excel have that other programs don't? For one, it has a built-in spreadsheet that you can manipulate the size and formatting. This versatile way of maneuvering the spreadsheet made it indispensable for many. Now, gone are the days were people have to manually draw tables in sheets of paper. Excel has already the tables prepared for them.

Another nifty feature of this software is its calculation function. Excel houses a myriad of formulas for solving arithmetic, financial and logical problems, among others. Thus, one doesn't even need to calculate every sum or average of a data series. Just by using a formula in Excel, everything can be done in an instant.

The Secret behind Mastering Excel

Speaking of instant, did you know that Excel has more than a hundred keyboard shortcuts? What does this mean to you as an Excel user? It means you can continuously work on your Excel spreadsheet without having to depend on your mouse constantly for Excel functions.

This is especially helpful whenever you are inputting a lot of data, and doing this will be more efficient if both of your hands weren't switching from keyboard to mouse and vice versa, every once in a while. In addition, if your mouse suddenly chose the most inopportune time to malfunction, learning Excel shortcuts can save you from major headaches.

As such, this book will provide you 100 keyboard shortcuts which you can use in Excel. In addition, as a bonus, you will learn about alternatives in case you forget any of these shortcuts.

Thanks again for purchasing this book, I hope you enjoy it!

Chapter 1: Moving Around the Excel Screen

People typically use the mouse for navigating the Excel screen. With this device, you can manipulate every cell in Excel, including its formatting and color. Since the mouse can access the major functions in Excel through the ribbon, there is no need for you to manually-type every formula or command.

However, the only difficult thing that you cannot do with a mouse is entering text. If you're going to use an on-screen keyboard, keying in the data in every cell would probably take you a lot longer than just using the keyboard for the text.

Thus, if you're going to use the keyboard most of the time, especially if you're just starting to build the spreadsheet data from scratch, it would be helpful to learn the basic keyboard shortcuts for moving around the Excel spreadsheet.

Shortcut #1: Arrow Keys

There are four arrow keys found in the right side of your main keyboard keys. These are the Arrow Left, Arrow Right, Arrow Up, and Arrow Down keys. Intuitively, you know that you can use these keys for moving within the spreadsheet. For instance, by selecting a cell then pressing Arrow Up, it will situate the cursor in the cell directly above your selected cell.

Shortcut #2: Ctrl + Arrow Key

Let's assume that you have a block of Excel data that spans more than 50,000 rows and more than 200 columns. You would probably have a hard time using a mouse in skimming these voluminous data. As such, you can use the Ctrl + Arrow key to navigate each "ends" of the data easily. In this example, click any cell in the block of data then press Ctrl + Arrow Down. You will be immediately located to the bottom cell in that specific column.

Shortcut #3: Shift + Arrow Key

You have selected all the items in the row but you forgot to include one cell. What would you do if you needed to include the next cell in the selection? Simply press Shift + Arrow Key, where the arrow pertains to the direction of the region you want to highlight.

Shortcut #4: Ctrl + Shift + Arrow Key

The above shortcut only includes one cell in the selection; but what would happen if you want to include everything until the last cell containing a data? You then use the Ctrl + Shift + Arrow Key.

Shortcut #5: Backspace

The Backspace key immediately deletes the contents of the active cell. However, if the cell is in Edit mode, it will only delete one character in the left of the insertion point, or the blinking cursor in the Formula bar.

Shortcut #6: Delete

This key has the same function as the Backspace key. However, instead of the left side, it removes a character in the right hand side of the insertion point.

Shortcut #7: End

Pressing the End key will enable the End Mode in Excel. In this mode, if you press an Arrow key, it will directly take you to the last used cell (or if none, last cell) in that specific direction. However, if the Scroll Lock is on, pressing the End key will only take you to the lower right corner of your Excel screen.

Shortcut #8: Ctrl + End

It works the same as the End key where pressing this combination will take you to the last used cell. However, if no cells were used, it will not move to the end of the worksheet like the End key does. Also, if the insertion point is located in the Formula bar (e.g., after the first character), Ctrl + End will put this cursor at the end of the field.

Shortcut #9: Ctrl + Shift + End

This keyboard shortcut can do two functions. First, in the Formula bar, it will select every character at the right of the insertion point. On the other hand, if you use it in the worksheet, it will highlight the cells starting from the active cell (or selected cell) until the last used cell in the worksheet.

Shortcut #10: Spacebar

Aside from putting a space in your text, it can also either select or clear a checkbox.

Shortcut #11: Ctrl + Spacebar

This will select the whole column to where the active cell is located.

Shortcut #12: Shift + Spacebar

It has the same function as the above, but this shortcut selects rows instead of columns.

Shortcut #13: Ctrl + Shift + Spacebar

Pressing these keys will select your entire worksheet.

Shortcut #14: Enter

After you have entered a data in a cell, pressing the Enter key will complete the input of data. Besides that, you can also directly go one cell below through this key. Considered as the most commonly used shortcut in Excel, you will be using the Enter key quite a lot because all Excel functions need it.

Shortcut #15: Shift + Enter

If you press Enter, you will go down one cell. Conversely, a Shift + Enter will complete an entry in a cell but the cursor will go directly above your entry.

Shortcut #16: Ctrl + Enter

Since this is a spreadsheet, it follows that after you have put an entry, you will enter another data below it. That is the common task whenever you're working on a table or database, which explains why the Enter key goes down. However, if you think that you need the downward movement, you can try Ctrl + Enter. This will plainly enter your data in the cell and it won't move your cursor to another direction.

Shortcut #17: Alt + Enter

You want the data to go into the next line in the same cell. However, if you press Enter, the cursor just moves on to the next cell in line. Pressing the Tab key doesn't work either. So what will you do? Try Alt + Enter key and see if it works.

Shortcut #18: Esc Key

The Escape key, or simply "Esc", performs a lot of nifty functions in Excel. Among of which are the following: 1) deletes a whole data in a cell, 2) exits you from a dialog box, and 3) escapes you from the full screen mode of Excel.

Shortcut #19: Home Key

The Home key will take you to the first cell in the specific row of your active cell. However, if the Scroll Lock is on, the cursor will go to the upper-left corner of your current window.

Shortcut #20: Ctrl + Home

This shortcut, also known as the "True Home key", brings the user to the beginning of the worksheet.

Shortcut #21: Ctrl + Shift + Home

This will select all cells from the active cell up to the first cell in the worksheet.

Shortcut #22: Page Down

Scouring among rows and rows of worksheets is now easy because of this button. This will display the next page in your Excel window.

Shortcut #23: Alt + Page Down

Unlike Page Down, the Alt + Page Down combination will show the next page to the right of your current window.

Shortcut #24: Ctrl + Page Down

Flipping in several worksheets is now easy thanks to Ctrl + Page Down. This will automatically turn you over to the next worksheet.

Shortcut #25: Ctrl + Shift + Page Down

The normal way of selecting several worksheets at once is to hold Ctrl while clicking each of the worksheets to be included in the selection. However, for those who don't think this is the practical way to do it, here's an alternative. Use the Ctrl + Shift + Page Down; it will automatically select the sheets for you.

Shortcut #26: Page Up

This is quite similar to Shortcut #22: Page Down key, except for the fact that this one goes in the opposite direction (which is upward).

Shortcut #27: Alt + Page Up

The Alt + Page Up will move your screen to the left, instead of right as what was described in Shortcut #23: Alt + Page Down.

Shortcut #28: Ctrl + Page Up

Same as Shortcut #24: Ctrl + Page Down, this will enable you to change sheets easily. However, this one goes in a counterclockwise direction.

Shortcut #29: Ctrl + Shift + Page Up

Selecting sheets is also a function of the Ctrl + Shift + Page Up. However, it will select the worksheets on the left hand side of your current sheet first.

Shortcut #30: Tab Key

Using the Tab key will enable you to move to the right hand side of the cell. Also, if you have a protected worksheet, pressing this can immediately take you to the next unlocked cell. Lastly, in case there is a dialog box, you can easily move along the options through the Tab key.

Shortcut #31: Shift + Tab

The Shift + Tab works the opposite way; if pressing Tab will take you to the right hand cell, this shortcut will locate the left cell for you. It also applies to the other functions of the Tab key. In a dialog box for instance, keying in Shift + Tab will move you to the previous option.

Shortcut #32: Ctrl + Tab

You're now done with shortcuts for moving around cells and worksheets. As such, the succeeding shortcuts in this chapter will focus on dialog boxes. For this shortcut, use it if you want to go to the next tab in a dialog box.

Shortcut #33: Ctrl + Shift + Tab

However, if you wish to go back to the previous tab in a dialog box, using the Ctrl + Shift + Tab is the right combination.

So there you have it, the first 33 keyboard shortcuts in Excel. Hopefully, through these tips you can know traverse in your multitude of cells and worksheets with no difficulty at all.

Chapter 2: Navigating the Excel Ribbon

Microsoft created the "ribbon" as a replacement to the expanding menus in the earlier versions of Microsoft Excel. It houses all the functions in Excel such as formatting, page layout, pictures, and shapes. However, since its interface is not in an expanding menu style, people are not that familiar with its keyboard shortcuts as compared to before where you can immediately see which shortcut runs which.

To help you with that, here are some of the most commonly used keyboard shortcuts for exploring the Ribbon.

Shortcut #34: Alt Key

Letters and numbers will appear in the ribbon once you push the Alt key. What happens is that it activates the access keys, wherein typing in corresponding letter or number will let you select a specific function in the ribbon.

Shortcut #35: F10

This key has the same function as the Alt key, only that pressing the F10 would require you to use your right hand instead.

Shortcut #36: Alt + Arrow Left/Right

To be able to navigate to the other tabs, use these keys.

Shortcut #37: F10 + Arrow Left/Right

Since it was previously mentioned that the F10 behaves the same way as the Alt key, pressing F10 followed by an arrow to the left or to the right will also transfer you to other tabs.

Shortcut #38: Ctrl + F1

There's no doubt that the ribbon indeed takes up quite a lot of space in your screen. Therefore, for those who want more area for their spreadsheet, hiding the ribbon is the best option. To do that, simply press Ctrl + F1. To show the ribbon again, also press the same shortcut.

Shortcut #39: Shift + F10

Shift + F10 is similar to the right click button of your mouse. It can open menus and other options depending on where your cursor is.

Shortcut #40: F6

You can move along three areas of the screen through this key. The F6 key, will take you either to the ribbon, the spreadsheet, or the status bar.

Shortcut #41: F10 + Tab

In a tab, you can browse through the functions by pressing this combination continuously. You can also press this shortcut first, and then proceed with the arrow keys for navigation.

Shortcut #42: F10 + Shift + Tab

The above shortcut goes around the functions in a clockwise manner. On the contrary, the F10 + Shift + Tab shortcut does otherwise.

Shortcut #43: F1

In the upper right corner of the ribbon, there is a blue question mark icon. Accessing this icon will take you to the Microsoft Excel Help task pane. Alternatively, if you press F1 the same pane will open.

Since the area around the ribbon is limited, it is only appropriate that there would be less keyboard shortcuts dedicated for it. All in all, there are ten button combinations for the ribbon.

Chapter 3: Formatting the Excel Spreadsheet

If you're also a user of the Microsoft Word, you are probably familiar with formatting keyboard shortcuts such as Ctrl + B, which stands for bold text or Ctrl + I, which italicizes your text. Since you can do almost every basic feature that you need in the Word application through the keyboard, this makes the formatting easier for you.

Fortunately, even though Excel is not a word-processing program, it also has dedicated keyboard shortcuts that for formatting. These are as follows:

Shortcut #44: Alt + '

By going to the Styles group in the Home tab, you can quickly change the appearance of the cell by selecting any of the pre-installed styles in Excel. To see the formatting changes done within a cell, you click on the New Style option, which will take you to the Style dialog box. Similarly, clicking Alt + ' will get you in the same menu.

Shortcut #45: Ctrl + B

Like in Microsoft Word, Ctrl + B will either apply or remove a bold format in a text.

Shortcut #46: Ctrl + 2

This shortcut can also make the selected text into a bold type.

Shortcut #47: Ctrl + I

Letter I stands for Italics. As such, clicking Ctrl + I will turn any text into an italicized type.

Shortcut #48: Ctrl + 3

This also functions like the Ctrl + I shortcut.

Shortcut #49: Ctrl + U

Ctrl + U will put an underline in the selected text.

Shortcut #50: Ctrl + 4

Another alternative for the Ctrl +U is the Ctrl + 4 shortcut.

Shortcut #51: Ctrl + 5

To easily put a strikethrough in your text, press Ctrl + 5.

Shortcut #52: Ctrl + Shift + F

If you want more font formatting options, you can just proceed to the Font tab of the Format cells dialog box. Right-clicking a cell then selecting Format Cells will get you there, or you can just use this shortcut.

Shortcut #53: Ctrl + Shift + P

This shortcut works the same as the above.

Shortcut #54: Ctrl + Shift + &

Now that you're done with editing the text, this shortcut as well as the succeeding ones will pertain to cell formatting. As for Ctrl + Shift + &, it will put a plain black border on all sides of the cell.

Shortcut #55: Ctrl + Shift + _

On the contrary, Ctrl + Shift + _ will remove the borders that you have made.

Shortcut #56: F4

Instead of manually doing all the formatting for a number of cells, Excel has a shortcut wherein you can redo the formatting that you just did in another cell. This is the F4 function key. For example, if you have put borders in Cell A1, selecting Cell A2 then pressing F4 will also create borders for that specific cell.

Shortcut #57: Ctrl + 1

Pressing the Ctrl + 1 will show the Format Cells dialog box. In this box, you can edit every possible formatting for a cell such as number format, alignment, font, border, and fill.

The previous chapters have discussed how certain shortcuts can perform specific functions in Excel such as formatting cells and navigating the spreadsheet. In the following chapters, the topics will be about the different uses of specific buttons such as the Function keys and the Control key.

Chapter 4: Working with Function Keys

The first row of keys in your keyboard contains the function keys, which is denoted by the letter F followed by a number. In the Windows desktop, these function keys can do a variety of tasks such as adjusting the screen brightness or minimizing the volume.

Excel uses the function keys for different purposes. Thus, most people usually have a difficulty mastering the Function key shortcuts in Excel.

Shortcut #58: Alt + F1

Alt + F1 will automatically create a chart for you. Just select the range of cells containing your chart data then press this shortcut. Afterwards, a column chart will appear in the worksheet.

Shortcut #59: Alt + Shift + F1

The normal way in creating a new worksheet is by right-clicking any of the existing worksheets then choosing Insert. The same task can be done by this shortcut.

Shortcut #60: F2

In editing a formula, you can't just simply select an active cell; you have to click on the Formula bar so that you can make changes to it. Fortunately, the F2 will put the cell in Edit mode. Thus, if you want to amend a cell, there's no need for you to click on the Formula bar; just use F2 instead.

Shortcut #61: Shift + F2

The Shift + F2 shortcut will insert comments in the active cell.

Shortcut #62: Ctrl + F2

Unlike the previous F2 combinations, this one has nothing to do with editing a cell. When you press Ctrl + F2, you will be forwarded to the Print Preview screen. Upon exiting this screen, your spreadsheet will show dotted lines which serves as a marker for a page border.

Shortcut #63: F3

Instead of constantly referring to a range of cells by their cell location (e.g., A1:D1), you can just define a name for this range. Thus, whenever you want to pertain to that specific range in a formula, you can simply put its name; there's no need for you to put the cell range. F3 will take you to the Paste Name dialog box, wherein you can list all the names created in a worksheet and their respective cell references.

Shortcut #64: Ctrl + F3

To create a new name, go to the Name Manager through Ctrl + F3.

Shortcut #65: Shift + F3

Using formulas is the heart of Microsoft Excel. Without it, you cannot do any calculations in the spreadsheet. As such, there is a dedicated tab for Formulas in the Excel ribbon. However, it may take quite a lot of time for users to efficiently look for the appropriate formula with all the possible options in the Formulas tab. Because of this, the Shift + F3 key combination is made. It opens the Insert Function dialog box, wherein you can easily search for a formula by just typing in the description of what you need to do.

Shortcut #66: Ctrl + F4

You don't need to click that "X" mark in the upper left corner of your Excel screen just to close the application; a simple Ctrl + F4 is enough to do the job.

Shortcut #67: F5

Rummaging through a lot of cells takes a lot of work, especially if you're dealing with thousands of rows in a spreadsheet. The Go To dialog box, which can be accessed through F5, will help you reach that specific cell or range that you wanted to see.

Shortcut #68: Ctrl + F5

By default, all workbooks are always in full screen mode in Excel. However, if you're doing work on several Excel files at once, it may be hard to switch from one file to the other when each workbook is on full screen. Through Ctrl + F5, the selected file restore to window size in the Excel screen so that you can easily switch across files.

Shortcut #69: Shift + F6

This works the same as Shortcut #40: F6, albeit in a counterclockwise direction.

Shortcut #70: Ctrl + F6

If you have more than one workbook open, pressing Ctrl + F6 will let you switch among these workbooks.

Shortcut #71: F7

Aside from Microsoft Word, the Excel application has also a built-in spell checker. To check the spelling of every word in your spreadsheet, press F7. This will run the Spelling dialog box. Apart from detecting erroneous spellings, it also suggests possible words that can replace the incorrect word.

Shortcut #72: Ctrl + F7

As mentioned before, you should not use the full screen mode when working with several Excel files. This is so that you can select each workbook with ease. The Ctrl + F7 shortcut executes the Move command so that you can drag the unneeded workbooks in another area in the Excel screen where it can't obstruct your view.

Shortcut #73: F8

Upon pressing F8, the Excel goes into an Extend Selection mode. This enables you to use the arrow keys to extend the current selection. Pressing the same key will also lift the Extend Selection mode.

Shortcut #74: Shift + F8

The limitation of the F8 key is that it only adds adjacent cells in the selection. Through Shift + F8, you can now add any nonadjacent cell by using arrow keys.

Shortcut #75: Ctrl + F8

To resize your workbook, use Ctrl + F8. This will run the Size command for workbooks that are not in a full screen mode.

Shortcut #76: Alt + F8

A macro is a set of actions created using the Visual Basic programming language. What it does is to automate a set of tasks in Excel. For example, you're going to retrieve a data in a one sheet then you'll paste the said data in another sheet. However, if you're going to do the copy-paste task for thousands of data, it might take you a long time. As such, you can use the macro for this. Alt + F8 will open the Macro dialog box, where you can record and run a macro.

Shortcut #77: F9

This is the Refresh button in Excel. Once you refresh a workbook, it will recalculate all new formulas in the said file.

Shortcut #78: Shift + F9

On the other hand, Shift + F9 will only recalculate the formulas in the worksheet you are currently working on.

Shortcut #79: Ctrl + Alt + F9

This has the same function as F9, but it will also recalculate formulas that have not been changed.

Shortcut #80: Ctrl + Alt + Shift + F9

Aside from doing what the Ctrl + Alt + F9 shortcut does, it also rechecks all dependent formulas for any errors.

Shortcut #81: Alt + Shift + F10

Smart tags are data that are labeled in a particular type. For instance, a person's name in an Outlook email message can be labeled with this tag. You can open the smart tag menu through this shortcut.

Shortcut #82: Ctrl + F10

This will enable a workbook to display in full screen mode (or maximized mode).

Shortcut #83: F11

The Shortcut #58: Alt + F1 will let you create charts by highlighting the data series. Similarly, the F11 key has the same function except that you don't need to select the data series; it will automatically detect the data for you. Another difference between these two shortcuts is that the Alt + F1 will display the chart in the same worksheet, while the F1 key will make another worksheet for the new chart.

Shortcut #84: Shift + F11

This is an alternative to Shortcut #59: Alt + Shift + F1, wherein it will insert a new worksheet.

Shortcut #85: Alt + F11

Alt + F11 will open the Microsoft Visual Basic Editor. In this menu, you can create or edit a macro by using the Visual Basic for Applications (VBA) programming language.

Shortcut #86: F12

The F12 key is the shortcut for the Save As dialog box. It lets you save your Excel file among the available formats.

In case you're wondering why the F1, F4, F6 and F10 keys as well as some of their derivatives are not included in the list, these function keys have already been discussed in the previous chapters. Moreover, as this book specifically claims that it will contain at least a hundred keyboard shortcuts, putting these function keys again in the list will not create an accurate count of all the shortcuts.

Chapter 5: Discovering Ctrl Combinations

There are more than 50 Ctrl key combinations that you can use in the Excel sheet, with some shortcuts comprising of special characters instead of the usual alphanumeric ones. Thus, it would be unpractical to include every possible shortcut, especially if there's a little chance that a typical user will use them all.

With these reasons, only the f14 most valuable Ctrl shortcuts will be contained in the list below.

Shortcut #87: Ctrl + ;

Ctrl + ; will show the current date in the active cell.

Shortcut #88: Ctrl + Shift + #

Ctrl + Shift + # will change the date into a day-month-year format.

Shortcut #89: Ctrl + A

This is an alternative to Shortcut #13: Ctrl + Shift + Spacebar. Pressing these keys will also select the whole worksheet.

Shortcut #90: Ctrl + C

Ctrl + C will copy the contents of the active cell.

Shortcut #91: Ctrl + F

If you need to search for a specific data, you don't have to go to the Home tab and choose Find & Select. By pressing Ctrl + F, you can now access the Find and Replace dialog box immediately.

Shortcut #92: Ctrl + K

To insert or edit a hyperlink, use this shortcut.

Shortcut #93: Ctrl + R

This activates the Fill Right command. To use this, simply click on a cell you want filled then press Ctrl + R. It will copy all the formatting and contents of the cell to its left.

Shortcut #94: Ctrl + S

Ctrl + S will automatically save your file in its current name, location and format.

Shortcut #95: Ctrl + V

After doing Shortcut #90: Ctrl + C, you then proceed with Ctrl + V to paste the contents that you have copied.

Shortcut #96: Ctrl + Alt + V

Since the above shortcut will paste all the data as is, the Ctrl + Alt + V will give you most pasting options as it will open the Paste Special dialog box.

Shortcut #97: Ctrl + W

This combination is an alternative to Shortcut #66: Ctrl + F4, which closes the Excel program.

Shortcut #98: Ctrl + X

This will cut the contents of an active cell. When you say "cut", it will remove the data in a cell and will place it temporarily in the Clipboard so that you can paste the contents in another cell.

Shortcut #99: Ctrl + Y

The Ctrl + Y shortcut runs the Redo function, which means that it will repeat the previous command that you have done.

Shortcut #100: Ctrl + Z

Lastly, Ctrl + Z serve as the shortcut for the Undo function. This will reverse your latest command in Excel.

And that finishes our countdown for the Top 100 keyboard shortcuts in Microsoft Excel. To wrap things up, the last chapter will provide some pointers in "memorizing" these shortcuts the easiest way.

Chapter 6: Pointers for the Excel Novice

Most people will most likely feel daunted with the mere volume of shortcuts in this book. "How can I ever memorize a hundred of these combinations?", says most people. This fear of memorization only impedes the learning process. As such, you should stay away from this negative thinking.

Practice a Couple of Shortcuts Every Week

To be able to remember these shortcuts effectively, you should use them as often as you could. Have this book by your side always so that you will have a guide as you try to absorb each of these shortcuts. Better yet, you can jot down a couple of shortcuts in a small list so that you can try some of these tricks in your school or the office.

After finishing let's say at least five shortcuts for a week, add another five in the succeeding weeks. Just don't forget the previous shortcuts that you have learned. In no time, you will be able to use these keyboard combinations without the help of a cheat sheet.

Don't Use the Numeric Keypad

Although most people on the go use laptops such as students, many people still use the full-sized keyboard that has a built-in numeric keypad at the right side.

Although several characters in the listed shortcuts are there, the Microsoft Excel does not recognize the use of numeric keypad in its shortcuts. As such, you shouldn't try to practice these shortcuts via the numeric keypad; just use the main keyboard itself.

That ends all the pointers in this guide for Excel shortcuts. With that, you should apply all the learnings that you have discovered through this book in your daily Excel tasks. Hopefully, you'll be a more efficient Excel user as you incorporate these shortcuts in using the said spreadsheet program.

Conclusion

Thank you again for purchasing this book!

I hope this book was able to help you to learn the secrets behind mastering Microsoft Excel, which are the 100 keyboard shortcuts.

The next step is to make use of these shortcuts every time you operate on the Excel application. Through this, you can now easily work on your Excel spreadsheets with only a minimal use of a mouse.

Finally, if you enjoyed this book, please take the time to share your thoughts and post a review on Amazon. We do our best to reach out to readers and provide the best value we can. Your positive review will help us achieve that. It'd be greatly appreciated!

Thank you and good luck!

Check Out My Other Books

Below you'll find some of my other popular books that are popular on Amazon and Kindle as well. Simply click on the links below to check them out. Alternatively, you can visit my author page on Amazon to see other work done by me.

C Programming Success in a Day

Android Programming in a Day

C ++ Programming Success in a Day

Python Programming in a Day

PHP Programming Professional Made Easy

HTML Professional Programming Made Easy

JavaScript Programming Made Easy

CSS Programming Professional Made Easy

Windows 8 Tips for Beginners

If the links do not work, for whatever reason, you can simply search for these titles on the Amazon website to find them.

www.ingramcontent.com/pod-product-compliance
Lightning Source LLC
Chambersburg PA
CBHW061042050326
40689CB00012B/2935